FOR THE LOVE OF

CATS

from **A** to **Z**

Written by **Sandy** *Robins* Illustrated and designed by **Mark** *Anderson*

Why do we love cats?

It's simple—they are the best companions in the world. And it's complicated, too. They are funny, curious, empathetic, independent (sometimes), and beautiful. At best, cats can teach us a thing or two about grooming, sleeping, and getting our own way. WILLIAM SHAKESPEARE REFERRED TO THEM IN THE *MERCHANT OF VENICE* AS "NECESSARY."

There's no need to ramble on here as this book has everything covered from A to Z with fun verses and informative factoids to improve your knowledge and impress your friends. It's for cat lovers young and old, the purr-fect gift for the cat person who has everything (except this book).

So why do we love cats...what's not to love?

"A" IS FOR

DORED

BY THE ANCIENT EGYPTIANS,

ACCORDING TO STATUES

AND ENTOMBED INSCRIPTIONS.

𝒰nlike other domestic animals such as the dog and the horse, the cat is self-domesticated. It's history shows that it chose to live in close proximity to people and this relationship dates back 10,000 years to the first settlers in Mesopotamia, the area also known as the Cradle of Civilization, in the Middle East. During the New Kingdom Era in Egypt some 3,000 years ago, cats were so adored by ancient Egyptians that they believed that the common cat was the reincarnation of Bast, the goddess of the fertility, love, pleasure, and dance and protector of all evil. Felines were so revered that the punishment for hurting or killing a cat was death.

The smallest feline is a masterpiece. —LEONARDO DA VINCI

"B" IS FOR

BREEDS

IN COLORS RED, WHITE, AND BLUE.

THE QUESTION TO ASK IS:

WHICH ONE IS FOR YOU?

There are about 80 different cat breeds recognized around the world. Different cat registries independently recognize different breeds. In the U.S., The International Cat Association (TICA) recognizes 55 breeds while the Cat Fanciers' Association (CFA) recognizes 41 breeds. Cat fanciers have their own "color palette" to describe coat colors. Red is commonly known as ginger or marmalade. "Blue" refers to gray. Lilac, lavender, and frost are all shades of light gray or dove gray. Chocolate is a dark rich brown and cinnamon is similar to the color of the spice. There is also special vocabulary to describe different coat patterns and shadings on the face (muzzle), paws, and tail. Learn more about the different cat breeds and their coat colors and markings at www.TICA.org and www.CFA.org.

"C" IS FOR

COMPANION.

AS THE WORLD'S MOST POPULAR PET,

CATS DEFINITELY ENJOY

ALL THE ATTENTION THEY GET.

There are an estimated 600 million cats in the world. According to an organization called The CATalyst Council, cats are ranked as the world's number one companion animals. Currently American cat lovers tend to have two or more cats per household, an idea supported by behaviorists who believe that cats thrive on the companionship of both humans and other cats. The power of the purr has been recognized by the medical profession to have wonderful soothing qualities, aiding patients both young and old. Consequently, felines are becoming popular therapy pets visiting assisted living centers, hospitals, and children's homes. The Delta Society is a national organization that evaluates and trains people and their cats to become pet partners and arranges for them to do therapy work on a regular basis.

"D" IS FOR OMAIN.

YOUR CAT OWNS YOUR FAVORITE CHAIR,

WHETHER IT'S VACANT

OR YOU'RE SITTING THERE.

*A*ll cats are, by nature, territorial. They have what's called a home range and a territory. A cat's home range is the area in which it is allowed to roam and, if allowed outdoors, can include quite a large area of the neighborhood. Its territory is much smaller and considered to be a safe environment with a plentiful food supply. So the food bowl is the very core of a cat's territory. Cats use scent messaging to stake their claim to an area. This is done in several ways; by rubbing up against an object using the scent glands on their paws or by chinning—rubbing the side of the mouth against an object. They do this to "claim" the people they love, too. They also use spraying urine and leaving feces as a method of leaving strong messages to other cats.

"E" IS FOR VENTS,

LIKE CHAMPION CAT SHOWS.

SOME LOVE THE PAMPERING

MORE THAN YOU KNOW.

Cat shows are held around the country every weekend. Whether it's a local, regional, or national show, the competition is fierce. Cat owners will spend hours grooming their cats at home beforehand and continue the grooming process right up until the moment their cat is presented to the judge. In America, most cat shows are held under the umbrella of The International Cat Association (TICA) or the Cat Fanciers' Association (CFA). Each has its own rules for judging and awards. However, from a spectator's viewpoint, both TICA and CFA organized events are set up along similar lines. Rows of cages (the benching area) house the feline participants waiting to be judged in a number of show rings, each presided over by a judge and a clerk to keep a record of the proceedings. The judging in the various rings goes on concurrently. Cat shows are often two-day events.

My cat's breath smells like cat food. —RALPH, THE SIMPSONS

"F" IS FOR

FINICKY

ESPECIALLY FOR FOOD.

BUT IF A CAT TURNS ITS NOSE UP,

DON'T THINK IT'S RUDE.

While cats are obligate carnivores, they sometimes have a palate for unusual tastes and will come and investigate the fruit and yogurt you are eating—or even your spaghetti Bolognese. Sometimes they appear to be turning their noses up at the food in the bowl but in fact they are "taste-scenting" their meal. There's an opening behind the nasal cavity that opens to the mouth called the Jacobson organ that allows them to taste-scent their food. To do this, the cat adopts a grimacing expression that appears as if it's turning up its nose in disgust. It's important to give each cat specially formulated foods to meet its specific dietary needs.

"G" IS FOR GAMES.

CATS LIKE TO PLAY A LOT

WITH PAPERS AND STRINGS

AND WHATEVER YOU'VE GOT.

Cats love to play games. Those that have an indoor lifestyle need to be compensated with lots of mental and physical stimulation in the form of toys and games. The pet industry has devised lots of wonderful playthings and activities to keep cats busy and, at the same time, hone their natural instincts to hunt. Engaging in play is a wonderful way to interact with your cat and establish a strong human-animal bond. Wands with fluttering objects on the end are excellent action toys. Distraction toys are those that will keep the cat engaged when home alone, for example a special track with a ball that spins around. Comfort toys include anything soft and cuddly for the cat to hunt and then carry around and possibly sleep next to. If you have a collection of toys, keep changing them around to keep things fresh.

"H" IS FOR HUNT.

CATS ARE BORN WITH THE SKILL

AND WILL CARRY ON STALKING

'TIL THEIR PREY IS STILL.

Cats have a natural instinct to hunt and fish. They play games around the home, tossing things around as if they are fishing or pouncing on things as if they are hunting real prey. It's their natural instincts at work in a domestic setting. The cat's hunting behavior is a classic sequence of stalking its prey silently and patiently before pouncing on it and playing with it to tire it. This is essential because cats are solitary hunters and need their prey to be in a submissive state so that they can finally move in with a kill bite to the neck.

*I*DENTIFICATION.

IN CASE THEY GET OUT,

IT'S A TICKET BACK HOME—

THAT'S WHAT IT'S ABOUT.

*C*ats get lost for a variety of reasons, from escaping through an open door or window to suddenly finding themselves stranded as a result of a natural disaster. Proper identification is a lost cat's ticket home. A microchip is the only form of pet identification that is permanent. It's a good idea for a cat to wear a collar and a tag, too. Cats that are out of their safe environment instantly go into survival mode and go silent to protect themselves from predators. Even the friendliest cat won't necessarily come when called. Depending on the cat's personality, they can remain close to home or travel within a five-block radius and hide for weeks. The best way of capturing a cat is with a humane baited trap.

A healthy cat can jump five times its own height.

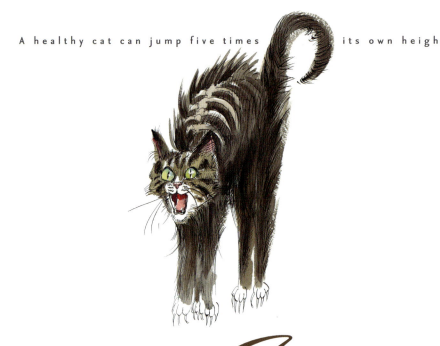

"J" IS FOR JUMP;

NOTHING'S OUT OF BOUNDS.

JUST WATCH THEM LEAP

IF THERE'S A HOUND AROUND.

Cats are natural jumpers and this innate agility allows them to escape out of trouble especially when being chased by predators. Sadly, through lack of exercise and bad diet, many cats are becoming couch potatoes; 40 percent of the feline population suffers from obesity. This impedes their ability to jump out of harm's way. However, as they age, even slim cats loose their ability to jump on to their favorite couch or bed. Help them maintain their independence by placing some pet steps alongside their favorite snooze zone so that they can access it on their own at all times.

"K" IS FOR *K*ITTENS.

AND WE KNOW FULL WELL,

WHEN IT COMES TO CAUSING CHAOS,

THEY CERTAINLY EXCEL.

*A*ll kittens are born with their eyes shut. Their inherent sense of smell and touch enables them instinctively to find their mothers and suckle. By the time they are two weeks old, their eyes have opened and their fur has begun to fluff out. At three weeks old, they are strong enough to begin walking about and continue to grow quickly. At four weeks, their ears are upright; they can stand properly with their little tails in the air. At six weeks old, they are very alert, their inherent curiosity becomes apparent, and they begin to take interest in small toys and everything around them, climbing on things and falling off. The great feline exploration has begun! Ideally, a kitten should be around 12 weeks old when it leaves its mother.

"**L**" IS FOR

*L*UCKY.

IT'S ALSO FOR NINE LIVES,

SURVIVING DEATH-DEFYING FEATS,

AND IMPOSSIBLY HIGH DIVES.

*S*ome believe the origin of this expression dates to ancient times when nine was considered a lucky number because it is the Trinity of Trinities. Feline resilience to injury led to the idea that cats have more than one life and thus the number nine seemed suited to describe a cat's survival rate. In terms of the laws of physics, a cat stands a greater chance of survival if it falls from a higher place than from a lower place. Any falling object, after traveling a certain distance through the air reaches a final speed, or "terminal velocity." Thus a cat falling from a higher floor, after it stops accelerating, spreads its legs into an umbrella shape, which increases the area against which the air must push and increases the friction, thus slowing its fall.

"M" IS FOR OVIE STARS

OF A FELINE KIND.

SLEWS OF REAL CATS AND CARTOON ONES

QUICKLY COME TO MIND.

When it comes to feline movie stars, there are many A-List contenders such as Snowball, the beautiful Persian that graced the lap of James Bond's archnemesis Ernst Stavro Blofeld in several Bond films including *From Russia with Love* and *Diamonds Are Forever*. In the Austin Powers spoofs of this famous series, a Sphynx cat named Mr. Bigglesworth accompanies his alter ego Dr. Evil. Garfield, the orange, lasagna-eating, Monday-hating tabby created by Jim Davis appears in more than 2,600 newspapers worldwide. This cartoon cat has spawned a merchandizing empire and also made several full-length feature films. When it comes to movie star cartoon characters, the list of funny felines includes Tom with his sidekick mouse Jerry and the lisping Sylvester with his most famous expression, "Sufferin' succotash!"

 IS FOR

 CAT WEEK,

EVERY NOVEMBER.

MAKE A NOTE TO YOURSELF—

BE SURE TO REMEMBER!

Cat lovers celebrate cats throughout the year. Important dates to remember include: January, National Cat Health Month, and February, National Dental Month. April 27 is National Hairball Awareness Day! The first week in May is Be Kind to Animals Week®, June is Adopt-a-Shelter Cat Month, and October 1 is National Feral Cat Day. The first week in November is National Cat Week and EVERY day is a Spay USA day—a program to provide low-cost spay and neutering promoted by the North Shore Animal League America. Local shelters and veterinarians work nationwide to promote these events that offer cat lovers various benefits, such as discounts on teeth cleaning services and lower rates for spaying and neutering, promote feline health and wellness, and provide cats with forever homes.

OJOS AZULES

ORIENTAL

o c i c a t

"O" IS FOR

OCICAT,

OJOS AZULES, AND THE ORIENTAL.

THEY ARE LIVELY AND FUN

AND NOT TEMPERAMENTAL.

Different cat breeds are known for their different characteristics and temperaments. Some, like the Siamese, are very talkative and love to follow their humans around engaging in games at every opportunity. The Abyssinian and the Turkish Van love water and, if given a chance, will join you in the shower. The Ragdoll is the quintessential lap cat. If you are considering a purebred cat, it's important to do your homework about the breed so that you are aware of typical breed personality and character traits to ensure that it will fit in perfectly with your family, home, and lifestyle. If you are adopting from a shelter, it's important to try and find out what the shelter knows about the cat's background and what life experiences it's had to date.

"P" IS FOR

ROWL AND POUNCE;

IT'S ALSO FOR PURR.

THAT'S WHAT CATS DO

WHEN YOU PET THEIR FUR.

Cats purr for a variety of reasons. For very young kittens, the purring sound emanating from their mother is like a soothing security blanket. They begin purring themselves when they are a couple of days old and it acts as a signal to the mother cat that her offspring are being properly fed. Throughout their lives, cats purr as a sign of general contentment. However, they also purr when they are in pain as the sound is soothing to themselves. The power of the purr also has therapeutic benefits for people. A 10-year study done by researchers at the University of Minnesota concluded that people who live with cats have a 40 percent lower chance of having a heart attack: living with a cat relieves stress and anxiety, common triggers for cardiovascular disease.

One cat just leads to another. —ERNEST HEMINGWAY

"Q" IS FOR

QUEEN,

WHAT THE FEMALE IS CALLED.

SHE'S REGAL AND FURRY,

EXCEPT FOR THE SPHYNX—SHE'S BALD!

A female cat is called a queen because when she is in heat, she rules over the tomcats courting her with regal autonomy. The feline gestation period is six or seven weeks and, on average, a queen produces two to four kittens per litter. Over the past 50 years, breeders have been working alongside geneticists to produce new breeds known as hybrid breeds. One of the most famous of these "designer" breeds is the Bengal, formed by the cross of a domestic cat with an Asian Leopard cat. Others include the Cheetoh (Ocicat and Bengal), the Savannah (domestic cat and a Serval), the Toyger (domestic cat and a Bengal), the Serengeti (Oriental cat and a Bengal), and a Chausie (a domestic cat with a Jungle cat). New breeds also develop as the result of natural mutations such as the tailless Manx cat and the Scottish Fold with its folded ears.

"R" IS FOR

*R*ESCUE;

THAT'S A GREAT THING TO DO.

A CAT WILL RECIPROCATE

BY LOVING ONLY YOU.

*I*t is estimated that between six and eight million cats and dogs enter animal shelters every year in the United States, but only about half of them make it out alive. Sadly, the rest, wonderful healthy pets, are euthanized to make room for others who are also in desperate need. Animal rights groups are working hard to curb pet overpopulation with spay and neutering programs and are striving to ultimately make America a no-kill country. Fortunately, there are independent rescue groups all over the country that take pets from city shelters and strive to find them forever homes. There are also specialized breed rescue groups. So if you are looking for a particular breed of cat, this is a great place to start. Google the cat breed you are looking for to find a breed rescue group in your area. Breeders are another good source of information.

"*S*" IS FOR

S LEEP AND SNOOZE.

FELINES DO IT A LOT,

WHETHER IT'S COLD

OR WHETHER IT'S HOT.

Cats sleep a lot, from "cat naps" to periods of deep sleep. The sleeping postures they adopt depend a lot on their size, body shape, and environmental temperature. A cat will sleep stretched out when it is hot and curled up in a ball with its tail wrapped around its curled body as a "muff" for extra warmth when it's cold. Elevated zones are always popular, such as on top of a cupboard or the top of a couch, where they can safely observe the household to ensure there will be no interruptions. Cats have a third eyelid known as the translucent nictitating membrane and when a shadow crosses it the cat instantly becomes alert and ready to spring into action.

Afraid

"T" IS FOR AIL;

Annoyed

CATS USE IT TO TALK.

IT'S DOWN WHEN THEY'RE WARY

AND UP WHEN THEY WALK.

Affectionate

Angry

Cats have very distinct body language using their tails, ears, eyes, whiskers, and body posture to communicate with each other and with people to divulge what they may be thinking or feeling. Here are some important translations for "tail talk": 1) An upright tail that quivers gently is a sign of happiness and excitement. 2) A slightly raised tail with a gentle curve means that something has piqued feline interest in a non-threatening way. 3) A gentle downward curve with the tip curled upwards is a sign of contentment. 4) A tail that is still except for the very tip, which twitches continuously, is an indicator that something is annoying or irritating the cat. 5) A tail that swishes from side to side in a fast motion denotes a very angry feline. 6) A fluffed-up tail carried low is a sign of fear.

"U" IS FOR *Urine*;

TO MARK A SPOT.

SOMETIMES IT'S BEHAVIORAL,

BUT SOMETIMES IT'S NOT.

*P*eeing outside the litter box is the number one reason cats lose their homes and land in shelters. The cat owner's first priority is to find the cause of such behavior. Often, it's a medical condition that can be cured with a trip to the vet. Cats will also pee outside a litter box if it's placed in a high-traffic area of the home, not kept fastidiously clean, and also if the box is too small. The rule is one litter box per cat in a household. Some cats even object to the type of litter used. Often the situation can be easily remedied. Peeing outside a litter box is very different from a male cat spraying around the home to mark his territory.

"V" IS FOR *Vacuum*

IN A WAR AGAINST FUR.

SOME RUN AND HIDE;

OTHERS JUST SIT AND PURR.

Shedding is a normal event in a cat's life. It's how they remove dead hair from their bodies and replenish their fur. Members of the cat family living in the wild usually shed twice a year: in the spring to remove their heavy winter undercoat and again in the fall in preparation of a new winter undercoat. However, domestic cats that are exposed to both air-conditioning and heating shed continuously. Shedding is largely influenced by daylight and determined by the number of hours a day that a cat is exposed to sunlight. This is called the photoperiod, which triggers the shedding process. The amount a cat sheds varies from breed to breed and also is affected by how often she is groomed. Consider grooming your cat as spending quality time together.

 IS FOR

 HISKERS.

FOR THOSE THAT ROAM,

THIS FELINE POSITIONING SYSTEM

GETS THEM BACK HOME.

A cat's whiskers are a highly sensitive guidance system that allows them to interpret distance, to tell if a gap is wide enough to pass through, to detect movement, and even to determine the shape of prey. Whiskers are enlarged stiffened hairs that are twice the thickness of ordinary hairs. They are also known as vibrissae. On average, cats have 24 whiskers in the facial area—twelve on each side of the nose arranged in four horizontal rows. They move forward when a cat is inquisitive about something and backwards when it is defensive or deliberately trying to avoid something. They also have reinforced hairs or whiskers on the underside of the forelegs to assist in stalking prey and to help judge landings. Whiskers are truly remarkable, hence the expression "the cat's whiskers" meaning something special.

"X" IS FOR

X-LARGE CATS:

LIONS, TIGERS, SNOW LEOPARDS, TOO.

THEY USUALLY LIVE IN THE WILD

BUT SOMETIMES LIVE IN A ZOO.

Domestic cats share many traits with their big cat Felidae family relatives, such as the manner in which they hunt, the poses they adopt, and even the way they manicure their toes. Big cats such as the cheetah and the snow leopard are on the endangered species list, and zoos throughout the world are instituting breeding programs to ensure their survival. Currently, researchers estimate that there are between 3,500 and 7,000 snow leopards left in the wild. No one has an exact count because snow leopards are so elusive and inhabit such harsh and remote habitat that they are rarely seen. There are about 600 of these cats in zoos around the world.

"Y" IS FOR *Yawn;*

IT'S A WAY OF SAYING *HELLO.*

IT'S ALSO A WAY OF SAYING

HEY! IT'S TIME TO GO.

Cat's yawn a lot; it's a form of greeting. If you walk into a room where your cat has been catnapping, you will more than likely be greeted by a yawn of recognition, with its mouth fully open and its tongue curled into a ladle shape. When a cat yawns in your presence, it's also a sign of trust and feeling comfortable in its surroundings. However, the feline yawn, just like words such as shalom and ciao which mean both hello and goodbye, can mean that the cat can't be bothered with anymore human interaction and it's time for another catnap.

"Z" IS FOR

ZORRO, ZIGGY, AND ZOE;

POPULAR NAMES ALL.

BUT IT DOESN'T MATTER—

CATS DON'T COME WHEN YOU CALL!

Actually, you can train a cat to come when called and to do many tricks, such as greeting you with a high five, shaking paws, and even playing "Three Blind Mice" on a piano. You can do this with clickertraining, which is a marker-based training method in which the trainer uses a handheld clicker to "click" and tell the cat that it has done the right thing and to instantly offer the cat a reward. The click identifies the behavior you plan to pay for with a treat the instant it happens. Cats are fast learners if you have the patience to teach them—and their favorite treats on hand!

The end

This book is available in quantity at special discounts for your group or organization. For further information, contact:

Triumph Books
542 South Dearborn Street, Suite 750
Chicago, Illinois 60605
312. 939. 3330
Fax 312. 663. 3557
www.triumphbooks.com

Printed in China
ISBN 978–1–60078–581–8